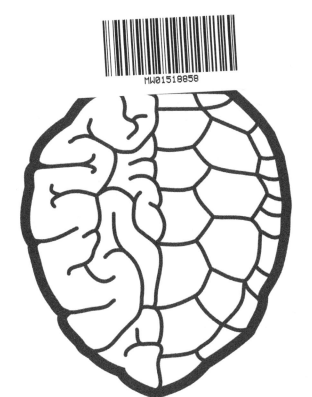

MW01518858

CHANGE YOUR MINDSET
CHANGE YOUR LIFE

First trade paperback edition: December 2017

Published and distributed by Create Space
www.createspacc.com

Cover Design by Maximo Lora
Illustration by Jonathan Rosales
Editing & Proofreading by Karen Wilder

ISBN-13: 978-1540392329

DEDICATION

I want to dedicate this book to my three beautiful sisters **Tiffany**, **Chelsea**, **Madison** and my creative brother **Aidan**. You are the reason why I strive for success. You are the reason why I learn from the best, to be the best that I can be so that I can pass the wisdom along.

My message to you and all my readers; All the power you need to accomplish anything is already inside you, all you have to do is believe and just do. I love you with all of my heart and mind.

Books| **Mindset Program** |Apparel

Congratulations On Purchasing This Book!

Below Is The Link To Create Your FREE Account To Access The Membership With Extra Content & Bonuses

SEA TURTLE MINDSET

A Journey of Self Discovery & Wisdom Traveling
The World

JONATHAN ROSALES

CONTENTS

FORWARD

Dear Reader,

I was going into my senior year at the University of Rhode Island when I decided to drop out. I worked for a couple of prestigious Civil Engineering companies, but I realized I didn't like the career. So I went to get a "real job" and became a personal banker for a top bank in New England. The first three months were fantastic, then the enthusiasm within the office dropped off and I began looking elsewhere. I have always kept myself open to options for making more money, be it full time or part time. While I was still working full time, I started to Uber part time.

Thank god I did. Uber changed my life.

After a couple months of working as an Uber driver, I was making more money part time than at my full time job. I was my own boss, I clocked in and out when I wanted, and I made as much money as I wanted. I got a taste of entrepreneurship, and around the same time, I joined a travel club. I felt inspired to go back to school and finish what I started.

On December 15th, I was a full time student and Uber driver when I took my first vacation with the travel club. I was jet lagged in Costa Rica at 5 a.m., and my English paper was due for submission on December 16th at 12 p.m. The task was to either recite a poem in class, or write a five page (double-spaced) short story. As I was out of the country, that pretty much made the short story my only option. So there I was, on the day before the assignment was due, just about to begin. Talk about Senior-itis at its finest!

But a funny thing happened when I sat down to write. The story just came to me. Three hours later, when I looked up for the first time, I had a 5 page (single-spaced!) short story with no conclusion. Looking at my laptop in the hotel suite, I decided to keep going. This story wanted to be a book. I felt sure of it.

And so this book was born.

The first two chapters are what I turned in as my final assignment. I earned an A in the class. I graduated spring 2016 and became a first generation college graduate.

Over the course of three years with the travel club, I took over 26 vacations, and this book was my constant companion. I would write on the airplane, in the hotel rooms, and on the beaches around the world. It felt fitting and inspired: as I was on my own journey, literally and metaphorically, I was spinning this tale of an epic life journey.

Exploring the world with my travel club opened my mind to dreaming and following my passions. I encourage you to do the same.

You are never too young to start an empire, and never too old to chase a new dream!

I am grateful to have the opportunity to share the wisdom I have gained traveling the world and experiencing different cultures. This book is the story of the lessons I've learned in my journey, yes— but it is my hope that you will feel a connection to your life and journey, too.

Sincerely,
Jonathan Rosales
Providence, Rhode Island

The Sea Turtle Mindset:

Consistency.

Persistence.

Repetition.

Continuously learning and practicing any skill until it becomes second nature.

YouTube Introduction Video
http://bit.ly/STMintroduction

CHAPTER 11

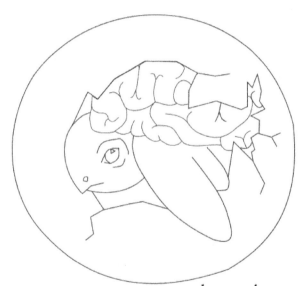

Are You A Land Turtle
Or A Sea Turtle?

"You're a Land Turtle, Aren't You?"

It's a beautiful Hawaiian afternoon, the sun is shining, and the sounds of the palm trees swaying in the sky play a harmonic melody. The birds are chirping along as a native plays, "Somewhere Over the Rainbow" on his ukulele.

A vibrant turquoise ocean rolls back and forth to the shoreline. A refreshing ocean mist travels on the breeze. The sound of the powerful waves crashing soothes the spirit. A feeling of tranquility emanates from the ocean's foam there on the beach as the waves trickle back to their source and seep into the sand.

When a castle stands upon pillars of sand, your foundation is everything. Digging a moat around his sand castle kingdom, seven-year-old Aulani is having fun in the sun.

Aulani has spent all morning working hard creating a firm foundation for his sand castles. Meanwhile, his mother sun bathes in nature's happy medicine.

As her child plays on the beaches of Hawaii, undiscovered truths lie in the vast ocean. It's the family's first trip to the tropical island of Hawaii, and so far, the sights have been breathtaking.

As Aulani collects sea shells to decorate his kingdom, he notices sand being tossed around off in the distance. With his little yellow bucket, he springs in that direction. Expecting to meet a new friend, perhaps building another sand castle, he is surprised to find a large green sea turtle.

Aulani keeps his distance. He lies on his stomach to observe the pit of sand. The sea turtle has laid her eggs and is now covering them with sand. She uses her rear flippers as shovels to hide the egg nest, wildly throwing sand in all directions. Some of the sand hits Aulani, covering him lightly.

In stealth mode, he patiently waits. Moments pass, and the mother begins to wobble her way back into the ocean. Aulani, fascinated by his first encounter with a sea turtle, wants to search for the eggs. He shakes off the sand, jumps right into the sand body pit left behind by the mother sea turtle, and begins to dig all around.

Unsuccessful at his first few attempts, Aulani does not quit searching. Diligent in his work, he at last finds the tear drop shaped nest. Overwhelmed by excitement, Aulani has found well over eighty eggs.

He sticks his hand in, feels the warmth of the eggs. He grabs the one at the top of the pile. Realizing that he needs to carry his egg back home safely, he fills his bucket halfway with sand. Then he places the egg in the middle of the bucket and covers the rest with sand. He covers up all the holes he dug out, and tosses sand all around just like the mother sea turtle did.

"Welcome to your castle, King Nori!" he proclaims as he wobbles back with the bucket.

"Mom! Mom! Mom! Look at what I found!" he shouts enthusiastically.

"What is it, baby?" she asks. "Some sand dollars?" She is smiling as she puts on her florescent green sunglasses.

Aulani looks up at her and sees his own smiling reflection. He says "No, silly! It's King Nori, my pet sea turtle. He is going to be the wisest of all Honu!"

Aulani's mother looks into the sand bucket and sees the unhatched egg.

"Oh, sweetheart—you can't take him away from his family. Go put him back where you found him." She looks at her watch. "Aulani, it's 12:17 p.m. We have to go register at the welcome table for our dream trip and meet Daddy at one o'clock for lunch." She begins to dust off the blue beach towel that says "You Should Be Here" and picks up his sand toys.

Disappointed, Aulani wobbles back in the direction of the nest where he found Nori. However, it looks different now. He can't remember the location of the covered nest. Looking around for any signs of turtles, Aulani spots a small herd of land turtles between the beach and the rainforest. His mother is calling for him. He quickly digs the egg out of his bucket and places it in the tortoise egg nest.

"Long live King Nori, the wisest sea turtle!" he says. He bends down to kiss the egg, then sprints back to his mother.

Cleaning her feet with the tides, she lifts Aulani to her hip. She holds him with one hand and carries the beach necessities with the other.

"Did you put the sea turtle back in its nest, baby? I'm sorry you couldn't take it home with you."

"It's okay, Mommy. A sea turtle's home is the world. They always find their life in the water because they love to swim forward."

"Well! How did you know that? That's very wise!" his mother says.

Aulani puffs up his little chest and smiles and kisses his mommy on the cheek.

Notes

_____

_____

_____

_____

_____

_____

_____

_____

_____

(Words of wisdom... this space is for you to record your "aha moments" making you
evolve from a passive reader into an active reader.)

#SeaTurtleMindset

YouTube Chapter Video
http://bit.ly/SeaTurtleMindsetChapter11

CHAPTER 10

Be Different

"Being Different Is What Makes You Unique"

Every morning when the sun rises, it's a unique brand new day, full of experiences and adventures. Every day the sky is painted with a variety of different colors and cloud shapes. It starts with shades of orange and purple, and it slowly becomes sky blue. Even the dark grey clouds rolling in from the east look marvelous on this particular unique day.

"Look! Look! It's moving!" one of the baby tortoises shouts as the last egg in the nest is hatching.

They all surrounded the egg, excited to meet their sibling. This egg is different from all the other eggs they had hatched from. It is a different color, shape, and size. As the egg begins to crack, they huddle closer to see. Out comes the head first, then slowly, the egg breaks all together. Shocked by the appearance of their newest sibling, the tortoises all step back.

"Why does he have flat feet?" one of them asks.

"Why does he have a flat shell?" another one follows.

"Hello, World! My name is Nori!" the baby hatchling says with joy in his voice.

Fearing the unknown, the tortoises are all scared into their shells.

"Why are you hiding in your shells?" Nori asks, confused. He has been looking forward to meeting his siblings.

"We hide to protect ourselves from danger," one of the baby tortoises says, his voice an echo from inside his shell. "We hide from things we are afraid of, like your flat feet and shell," another one adds.

"Well, the good news is I'm not dangerous, but what happens if it's a real threat? What if it never leaves? Will you hide in your shell forever?" Nori asks.

"You're right! I'm not afraid of you!" the biggest tortoise in the group says as he comes out of his shell. "You're just weird looking!" he says, laughing. They all begin to laugh as they come out of their shells.

"Hey, flat feet!"

"Hide in your shell, flat feet!"

"Oh, we forgot—you cannot hide in your flat shell!"

These negative comments frustrate the young sea turtle. He wants to immediately seek an explanation as to why he has hatched as a creature so different from his siblings. He wobbles his way to his mother.

Protecting her newly laid eggs, her body is seclusive while she sleeps. She has short, stumpy legs with claws that help her move around, and as Nori approaches, they pop out from beneath her shell. Her dark brown skinhead and shell decorated with scale-like shapes rises up. Nori's flippers make a flapping sound on the road.

"Mom, why was I born different from everyone else?"

"Baby, being different is a blessing. It means you are unique, and there is nothing wrong with being different."

"But the others are afraid of me, and it makes me angry. They also started to call me names like 'flat feet'."

"Listen, my son, it does not matter what others TH!NK of you. What is important is what you TH!NK of yourself. As long as you love yourself for who you are, you don't need to listen to the opinions of others. The elders always told me, 'If you value someone's opinion, be prepared to live their lifestyle. Use that anger and channel it as motivation."

She gives Nori a warm smile. He thinks about that last word: *motivation*. What might that mean?

"Why can't I hide in my shell like the other turtles?" he asks.

"The answer to that, I do not know, my son. My advice to you is to seek the wisdom of the eldest. Elder Tortuga. He knows more than any turtle I know. Maybe he can answer the questions you have. He lives upland not too far from here."

But I don't want to go upland, Nori thinks. *I just want to fit in so I can play with my siblings.*

After only a moment, though, Nori realizes his desire to learn more about himself is far greater than his desire to fit in.

As he wobbles upland, he is taking his first steps toward self-discovery. He does not know this, of course. He is just a little hatchling. But even a hatchling can find himself on a quest.

And so begins Nori's quest to discover the reason for his uniqueness, and to learn who he really is.

Notes

_____

_____

_____

_____

_____

_____

_____

_____

_____

(Words of wisdom… congratulations for getting this far! Statistics say that most books
are never read passed the first chapter, keep on growing!"

#SeaTurtleMindset

YouTube Chapter Video
http://bit.ly/SeaTurtleMindsetChapter10

CHAPTER 9

Knowledge Seeker

"Seek The Wisdom Of Mentors"

Unlike the others, Nori has long green flippers, not short stumpy legs. This makes him wobble. He moves more slowly than the rest, but when he sets out to do things that he wants to do, he doesn't quit! Slowly but surely, Nori reaches Elder Tortuga.

Much larger in size than most of the tortoises in the herd, Elder Tortuga's shell has pyramid-shape scales that rise high above his head. This eldest tortoise is about 80 years old, and the different scars on his back give him a very rusty look. His long neck sticks out, and his scaly brown stump legs are each the size of Nori. He is sunbathing under the warm sun, as a storm gathers on the horizon.

"Hello, Elder Tortuga! My name is Nori, and I came to seek your wisdom."

"Who said that? Where is that tiny little voice coming from?" he says with a slow, rusty look around.

"Down here!!!" Nori yells as he flaps his flipper up and down.

"Ohh, a little one! Hello, squirt. You made a journey to me for my wisdom, you say? To seek knowledge makes you stand on the carapace of the Aldabra giant tortoises, which will help you see further than others. For your courage and efforts to seek my knowledge, I shall answer the questions you bring to me today."

Nori asks his first question:

"Why did I hatch so different from the rest of the tortoises?"

"There is nothing wrong with being different, young one."

"So, why can't I hide in my shell like the others?" Nori politely asks the elder

"Would you rather hide away from your fears inside your comfy warm shell, or face your fears by handling pressure and getting uncomfortable?"

"I want to do both: hide away like the others and manage my fears with pressure." Nori innocently responds to his elder.

"Listen, my young student, you can either have excuses or results, but you can't have both. I will tell you something: if you hide away from your fears, they will never go away. You will come out eventually and guess what? They will still be there! All you are doing is neglecting."

Nori considers this as Elder Tortuga goes on.

"On the bright side, when you handle the pressure from your fears, you become immune to those fears!

Get uncomfortable and fight back against those fears, that's what I always advise. Besides, green sea turtles can't hide in their shell!" He bursts out into laughter, then continues with a wise old sea turtle grin. "Being reclusive is a waste of time, and your species can handle more pressure than you imagine."

"A sea turtle? Is that what I am?" Nori ponders this.

"Yes, a sea turtle! I'm a land turtle, or one might say, a tortoise." He looks around to see if anyone is listening. He lowers his voice and leans in toward Nori. "I would rather be a sea turtle," he confides, as he chuckles at the idea.

Nori is genuinely surprised.

"Why would you rather be a sea turtle, Elder Tortuga?"

"Well, for starters you have the ability to travel all around the world. When you travel, you get to experience new waters, meet different creatures, and claim the vastness of the world as your playground. That's quite impressive, is it not?"

Nori nods, considering this idea. The whole world as his playground? The thought is thrilling!

"The second reason I would rather be a sea turtle is that you are going to grow vast in size, even bigger than me!"

Nori looks down at his tiny flippers, then up at the massive tortoise. It seems impossible that he will grow bigger than Elder Tortuga, but he imagines it must be so. Wisdom can't be wrong.

"Where will I go?" Nori asks.

"Wherever your heart leads you."

"What am I searching for?"

"You are searching for your true self. The thing that drives you inside. The spark that ignites you to wake up every day, and makes you hungry for more."

Nori tips his head skeptically. He's not sure he's felt a spark. But then he considers the journey he's just made to find Elder Tortuga. *Something* drove him to do that. Something beyond his mother's words. Could this be what the old tortoise means?

"How will I know if I'm going the right way?"

"Listen to your heart first, and then your mind, and you will just know."

"What if I get lost? How will I navigate around the world all by myself?"

"Whenever you feel lost, just look up and your answers will be given to you. The stars will always help you navigate across the oceans when you are aiming for them."

Nori feels truly confused. Why would he be aiming for the stars while he navigates the ocean? Still, Elder Tortuga must know. Nori commits the instruction to memory.

"What do I do when I find my true self?" he asks at last.

"Get excited, pay attention, and never quit. As you travel through life, you will discover the infinite abundance of this world. It is your birthright. Having more room to live allows more room to grow. Do what you love, and you will live an amazing life."

"Doing what I love sounds easy," Nori laughs.

"Don't be confused, young one. I never said life was easy, or that doing what you love is going to be easy. It is going to be hard work with long hours. Yes, doubts will come and distractions will delay you, but you must remain self-disciplined. Doing what you love won't be easy, but it will be worth it."

"Okay fine," Nori says, though he's not sure he sees how doing what he loves could ever be difficult, "It won't be easy, but what if I find short cuts along the journey?"

"Ah, young one, listen to me well on this point: ***there are no shortcuts in life***. However, when you commit to a single task every day consistently over a long period of time, the compound effect may feel like a shortcut. A journey of a thousand miles begins with a single step, and it *finishes with a single step*. Or in your case, a single thrust of your flipper." Elder Tortuga laughs, but Nori feels a new concern creep in.

"What if I am not strong enough?"

"Ah, young Nori, you are stronger than you imagine. I have about a hundred scars, each one with a story to tell. The deeper they are, the harder they healed. The more scars I've earned, the stronger I've become. I have learned that truly, without pain there is no gain. Pain is the action one undertakes to become stronger than the turtle you see in your own reflection. You will have your failures, but for every failure there is an equal amount of success. Learn from your mistakes and swim forward. Just do the thing each day that you know you must do, and you shall have the power."

Nori ponders this. He does not like the idea of pain. It begins to rain softly. His shell shines bright green with the moisture.

"What if I sink down to the bottom?" Nori asks.

"Listen, my small friend, we could sit here and discuss all of these "what ifs" all day long. But they are limiting your ability to succeed. Worries come from doubt. If you keep worrying and trying to grab hold of all the answers, you will sink and drown. You must have faith, and it must be unwavering."

"Faith?" Nori muses. "What is faith, and how do I get it?"

"Faith is like trusting yourself in the water. To swim, you don't grab hold of the water, all you do is relax and float. You already know how to swim. If you try to grab hold of the water you will sink and drown. Just relax and be like the water. Always move forward. The more you learn, the more you will grow."

"What about..." Nori begins, but he is cut short by a loud thunderbolt striking a nearby palm tree.

Elder Tortuga quickly hides in his shell, startled. He looks out at Nori, and sees no fear in his little eyes. He meets the sea turtle's gaze as he emerges slowly from his shell.

"Young Nori," the elder smiles in his gentle voice, "I think you may have learned all you need to know from me. If you seek more answers, I recommend seeking the wisdom of the wisest and oldest tortoise alive in the world. Rumor has it that The Great Jonathan is still alive, and he lives on a tropical island like ours, called Saint Helena. It is off the West coast of South Africa. I am certain that his 187 years of wisdom shall afford answers to any further questions you have."

Notes

_____

_____

_____

_____

_____

_____

_____

_____

(Words of wisdom… if you record your "aha" moments while reading, you will
remember and retain more by being an active reader)

#SeaTurtleMindset

YouTube Chapter Video
http://bit.ly/SeaTurtleMindsetChapter9

CHAPTER 8

W.I.T.

"Do Whatever It Takes To Conquer Tides"

Suddenly, the light rainfall turns into a downpour from the heavens. Nori feels refreshed, mentally and physically. He swiftly glides down the streams of water down the mountain.

Downland he goes, toward the sea shore where the herd resides. In his search for the others, Nori realizes that they have all gone to highlands. His mother has remained behind, waiting for him.

"Mom! Mom! Listen to what I discovered about myself: I am a Sea Turtle!"

"I told you my son, there is nothing wrong with being different," she says, standing tall with her brown neck extended. "Better that than being the same. Life with everything and everyone the same would be very boring indeed!"

Nori looks at his mother, there in her dark brown shell that resembles the Hawaiian mountains, and feels a surge of love.

"I am at ease in my own shell, and I thank you for seeing the greatness in me even when I didn't," Nori tells her. "Elder Tortuga gave me many answers, but now I have more questions, too. I have decided to go on a journey to seek the wisdom of The Great Jonathan. It is an idea that made me feel a..." he pauses, trying to recall the word his elder used, "spark! Yes, that's it—I feel driven to go. I want to learn from Jonathan. I will be the wisest sea turtle who has ever lived."

"I believe in you Nori," his mother encourages him. "The day you cross the ocean and lose sight of the shore is the day you will gain courage! Remember that direction is so much more important than speed. No matter how slow you may be going, as long as you never quit, it is better than going fast nowhere. And remember, there is nothing impossible—because YOU are possible! Now, GO! I love you!"

Determined, Nori heads towards the sea. As he crosses the beach, rain is pouring down. The sky is gray, the wind is blowing at intense speeds, and giant waves are crashing upon the shore. Nori stops halfway, his little heart pounding against his plastron.

He quickly wobbles and sticks his neck out as far as he can repeating, "There is nothing impossible, I am possible! There is nothing impossible, I am possible! There is nothing impossible, I am possible!"

Taking a deep breath, he dives into the sea. There—he's done it! Letting out a sigh of relief, he gains more momentum while in the water.

Not knowing the power of the ocean, he catches his first wave late and gets wiped out. Even though waves are crashing down and currents are pulling him back to shore, he doesn't quit. He paddles as hard as he can.

Tossed around by the wave he finds himself back on the beach. Nevertheless, he sets out once again. Impatient to be back on his way, he catches the next wave late and gets wiped out a second time. After several failed attempts, he finally steps back to analyze.

His first instinct is to say, *I just can't do this,* but he knows neither his mother nor Elder Tortuga would approve of that sort of thinking. So instead, he asks himself, *How* **can** *I do this?*

His little turtle brain starts cranking out different ideas and possibilities. It feels a little bit like asking Elder Tortuga to share his wisdom. Nori suddenly understands that asking yourself good questions creates windows of opportunity.

There is always another wave. If he catches the wave late, Nori realizes, he gets wiped out. Time and again. But as he searches the sea, he notices a pattern. He gets himself into position, and patiently, he waits. As soon as the next wave crashes, he jumps in and begins to thrust his green flippers.

All he keeps TH!NKING about is his burning desire for wisdom from the great one.

He keeps swimming, thrusting one flipper at a time, swimming and thrusting, one flipper at a time, swimming and thrusting. After what seems like an eternity, he is finally far from the shore. He is out of the churning surf, and is surrounded by the stillness of the vast, calm ocean.

He opens his eyes underwater for the first time and sees he is surrounded by countless shades of blue. He looks up to the surface of the water, notices how the drops of water look like pebbles falling from the sky. Each small drop collectively increases the size of the ocean. The power of the waves crashing at the shore is magnificent, but beneath the surface of this massive living entity, the quiet elegance is breathtaking.

A feeling of tranquility fills Nori. A keen sense of self-awareness washes over his baby sea turtle shell. He is one with the ocean. He is where he is supposed to be. His awkwardness on land was just because a sea turtle was made to be, well, in the sea!

Nori swims to the surface, takes a deep breath, and looks back at the shore. It's not about where you started, he thinks, or where you are right now. It's about where you are going.

Nori realizes that is something of a problem. He knows he needs to find The Great Jonathan, and he knows the name of the place where he lives, but he has not the slightest clue how to get there, or how he will sustain himself on his journey.

The sky begins to clear up, and Nori hears the sounds of seagulls high up in the air. He can hear the waves softly crashing onto the beach. He does a little dive, delighted with how his body moves so easily through the water.

He TH!NKS to himself, "I will either figure out a way, or create my own way!"

With this mindset, the little green sea turtle begins to swim. He swims, and swims, and swims until he loses sight of the shore.

Notes

_____

_____

_____

_____

_____

_____

_____

_____

(Words of wisdom... if you use a blue ink pen, studies have shown your brain will remember new concepts more)

#SeaTurtleMindset

YouTube Chapter Video
http://bit.ly/SeaTurtleMindstChapter8

CHAPTER 7

EMBRACE

PRESSURE

"Heat + Pressure + Time = Diamonds"

Twenty years pass.

Nori has traveled thousands of miles in the Pacific Ocean, from Hawaii to the Philippines. He has even found himself in the waters around Japan. He has met countless creatures and learned the names and seascapes of many places.

Continuously learning and with constant, never-ending dedication to his own improvement, Nori becomes wiser day by day. One day, he is practicing his deep sea diving techniques. He wants to be able to journey to tremendous depths.

"Are you ready to get started, Nori?" asks Maximus, the great leatherback sea turtle.

He deep dives into the Pacific Ocean off the coast of Costa Rica. Nori has spent almost two decades with the great leatherback mentor, learning how to feed and defend himself in the North Pacific ocean.

They have traveled together far distances, helping each other grow and learn. Maximus is twice Nori's age, and though Nori's size has increased tremendously, he is still smaller than his friend, whose shell spans six feet. They have been practicing deep sea diving for years.

"Are you sure my shell can handle the pressure?!" Nori calls out.

His friend is diving down into a cave, and all Nori can see is his large inky-blue carapace with its unique pattern resembling waves.

"Listen up!" Maximus calls back. "This is what we have been training for! Practice makes permanent! You came to me as a squirt, and now look at you— you have grown vast in size and in knowledge. The cave you fear to enter may be the cave in which you become mighty! You can do this! I believe in you!"

Nori swims to the surface, takes a deep breath. He TH!NKS to himself, "Massive immediate action is the foundation to all success." He has learned this is true.

With this thought, he dives deep into the infinite waters. With a sudden burst of speed, he reaches one thousand feet, two thousand feet, and finally three thousand feet! On the way down, he steadily passes his mentor. He arrives at the entrance to the cave. Maximus goes in first, and Nori follows him without hesitation.

"Magnificent, aren't they?" Maximus asks him.

"*What are they?*" Nori stares at the shiny rocks all around the inner wall of the cave. Rays of the sun filter down through a small opening at the top of the underwater cave. The thin beam of light shines through the darkness and hits one of the rocks, causing a prism effect. The entire cave is lit up with a brilliant turquoise color.

"Humans call them diamonds, my friend, these beautiful rocks. Do you know why I brought you here?" Maximus asks Nori, looking nostalgic. The small green sea turtle has grown to over four feet in size, and his shell is covered with patches of algae from the coral reefs the two friends have swum through.

"You are testing me to see if I can handle the pressure?" Nori tries. "You have taught me everything a green sea turtle can do, and I have gained leatherback qualities through the lessons."

"True, but do you know how diamonds are formed, Nori?" Maximus asks.

"No, sir," Nori says, eager to learn.

"Diamonds first start as coal, an ugly chunk of brownish-black rock found in sea cliffs. They do not turn into diamonds overnight. There are three components that are required for transformation:

"The first component is intense heat. Heat is the transfer of energy from an object to its surroundings or to an object from its surroundings—in this case the chunk of coal. This same heat expands the object either positively or negatively. When you're heating up in your life, you're just getting started.

"The second component is pressure. In the case of diamonds, this is the continuous force exerted against the surface of the coal. You can either be exerting the pressure, or be under pressure. However, you must be patient. Applying heat and pressure on your goals is not enough.

"The final component is time. Time can be our enemy if treated unwisely, or our friend if treated well. Time is the only luxury and the most precious resource we all have. When I TH!NK of time, I TH!NK about *T*hings *I M*ust *E*arn."

"Time is like the tide, it waits for no sea turtle," Nori says. He gazes at the diamonds and smiles at his reflection.

"Fantastic job, you learn fast," Maximus says. "Without any heat or pressure over a season of time, you will only have a chunk of coal as a result of your efforts."

"You have been patient with me throughout these years. I have noticed when dealing with pressure, it doesn't matter how long it takes you to master it. What matters is that you never stop working on it. Sometimes I doubt myself, but it is my inner desire to become the wisest that pushes me to gain higher levels of awareness."

Maximus swims up to the top of the cave, and covers the hole where the light enters. They are now in total darkness. Nori feels the captivating silence that surrounds him. All he can hear are his own thoughts, all he can feel is tranquility within the darkness of the ocean cave.

"Okay, my young friend—before I let you go on your own journey to meet the Great Jonathan and learn from his wisdom, I have one last lesson for you," Maximus says from the top of the cave.

"Okay!" Nori calls in response. "Just like the coal that under tremendous pressure and over a long period of time turns into a diamond, I am ready for my transformation!"

"When you are surrounded by darkness," Maximus asks him, "how do you find the light?"

"By never losing faith," Nori responds without hesitation. "If you have faith, you will never be consumed by the darkness, so long as you consistently intensify your desire to push forward, the light of certainty shall lead the way out." Nori swims down and floats at the entrance of the cave.

"Life is the greatest teacher of all, Nori," Maximus affirms as he moves to shed light back into the cave. "It is like the ocean current. It will constantly test you by pushing you around. Each push is the ocean telling you to keep swimming. Either you are washed away by the current, or you swim stronger on the crest of the wave. The way you ride the current determines your destination. You have been, as the

Costa Rican sea turtles say, "Pura Vida," a fantastic and marvelous student."

"I can't thank you enough for teaching me most everything I've learned so far," Nori responds. "I feel so much more confident in my ability to take on the world." Nori exits the cave and pauses, turning back to his mentor. "See you later, my dear friend!"

Nori swims to the surface of the ocean, and he takes a deep breath of fresh air.

The sun is shining bright on a late Pacific Ocean afternoon. Nori has the beach shore within sight, but this time it is not from Honolulu, but Costa Rica. The shores of Tortuga Island are located in the Gulf of Nicoya. Palm trees and overgrown jungles fill the island. The coral reefs in the area are full of life and diversity.

The beauty of the ocean is magnificent. Nori swims through the coral reefs surround by a variety of colorful fishes and delicious green seaweed. The sun is the source of energy for the rainforest of the sea. All the animals that live in the coral reefs balance each other.

As Nori is minding his own business, which most sea turtles do, he realizes all the fish have begun to rapidly swim away from the feeding area. He notices some stripes on a gray fish approaching, but he continues to enjoy his meal with no worries. Then his sensitive shell feels pressure...

""Hey! HEY! What are you doing?" Nori yells. Slowly, he realizes that a tiger shark has taken a bite of his shell. The shark attempts another bite on his shell, and Nori suddenly feels a spike of pain from his left back flipper. He realizes he doesn't have a second to spare, but instead of panicking and fearing the attack, he remembers an important lesson from Maximus, "Be at ease in your own shell, and you shall find a way."

With this in mind, he swims in a circle formation, turns on his side, and uses his shell as a shield. When the shark swims at full speed, Nori swiftly dodges the attack. Persistently, the shark maneuvers to the injured flipper, but Nori quickly uses his strong jaw, and bites the shark's body. The sea turtle mindset is an agile one compared to a full force shark mentality.

The sharp-toothed predator is eager to have Nori as his meal, but the crafty sea turtle continues to use the same winning strategy. This time he clutches the shark's tail with his jaw. Overcome with frustration, the shark shakes loose, and flees.

Nori lets out a cheer. Not only has he escaped becoming the shark's dinner, he has gained a valuable sense of his own strength. "That is the adversity I needed! If you stay prepared and ready for the difficult times when it is easy, you don't need to get ready!"

Exhausted from the shark encounter, Nori swims toward the shore. His flipper begins to ache as he swims in the shallow water. He wobbles onto land, and beach sand begins to irritate the bite. He takes his rest as the sunset paints a beautiful sky of orange and purple clouds.

Nori feels a pang of nostalgia for the first time he felt soft and warm sand beneath him. Instead of white sand, he was on black sand then. He was a sea turtle who thought he was a land turtle. His mother encouraged him to seek wisdom, and he learned the truth that set him off on his amazing journey. The zealous attitude he had as a baby sea turtle grew into the mindset that has served him well all his life.

Nori nurses his wounded flipper and thinks of how important that mindset has proven to be. He always believed in himself, no matter the obstacles laid in his path. Today, that belief saved his life.

As the last of sunset turns to dusk, Nori whispers his old affirmation to himself:

"There is nothing impossible, I am possible!"

Notes

_____

_____

_____

_____

_____

_____

_____

_____

_____

(Words of wisdom... underline and mark the portions of the book that are meaningful to you, personalize it and record your thoughts, this will make it "your" book.)

#SeaTurtleMindset

YouTube Chapter Video
http://bit.ly/SeaTurtleMindsetChapter7

CHAPTER 6

"Knowledge, Strategize & Implement"

Months pass as Nori swims in the vast ocean. His flipper heals, leaving the mark of a battle scar. He does not look back in anger at the incident with the shark, nor forward in fear of another shark attack, but around with awareness. After accepting and letting go of the past, Nori has pushed forward with more courage in the present.

In the wake of a tropical storm, the sky slowly begins to open up, and the sun's rays break through the clouds. At a distance, Nori hears echoes. They become louder and louder. The echoes are not unpleasant, but they are strange, and they're bouncing off his shell in series of three. He keeps swimming harder to get away. Nevertheless, they seem to get closer.

Suddenly he stops swimming and TH!NKS to himself: "A brave turtle is not paralyzed by fear, but instead is eager to conquer that fear." He swims up, breaking the surface of the ocean. He takes a deep breath, trying to relax and focus. He sees three shark fins approaching. "What you fear the most will help you gain strength, courage, and confidence once you look that fear in the face!" he reminds himself.

As they approach, coming closer and closer, the echoes suddenly disappear. Drawing in another breath of air, Nori says to himself, "I have lived through this experience before. I can take the next thing that comes along. You must do the thing you TH!NK you cannot do."

Submerging under the water, he begins to swim in the direction of the sharks. Nori quickly picks up speed so that he can catch them off guard with a shell clash.

Nori slams into the first in line and screams!, "AOOOWWW!"

After the clash, he notices that these three creatures are not sharks, but in fact, dolphins.

"Hey! Why did you just slam into my brother Socrates?" one of the dolphins asks Nori, "Are you a mad sea turtle?"

"I apologize tremendously," Nori says quickly. "I acknowledge that I am at fault. I assumed that you were sharks! Your back fin confused me and made me fight my fears instead of fleeing. Again, I am so very sorry!"

"Apology accepted, young one," the injured dolphin replies in a kind manner. "It takes a lot of strength to acknowledge your flaws. We apologize if we startled you, but we're surprised to have located a sea turtle traveling alone so far from any source of food at this time of year."

"Yes, I understand," Nori says, "I have found that traveling alone stretches my mind. I'm fascinated by my own thoughts. On my journey of self discovery, I've learned how to speak to myself in a loving way. Even when I mistake dolphins for sharks."

The dolphins chuckle along with Nori.

That is very noble of you," one of them replies. "My name is Plato, my friend. My other brother is Aristotle, and your shell met with Socrates' nose."

All three dolphins dissolve in laughter again.

"My name is Nori," the sea turtle introduces himself. "It is a pleasure to meet you three. I have heard stories from my fellow sea turtles. They say that dolphins are very intelligent." Nori compliments the brothers with curiosity in his tone. He is eager to learn from them.

"Is this knowledge stored in your mind as a fact?" Socrates asks as he does a flip out the water.

"I use the storage of my mind to TH!NK. That space is for dreams, and for knowledge to be put to use."

"Ah Plato, look at how this young turtle's mind has grown! What do you have to say to him?" Socrates emits echo pulses that are gentle and sweet.

"Nori, you understand that *knowledge* is only power when applied—so how do you plan for your outcomes and results?" Plato asks, swimming around the sea turtle.

"What I have learned so far, Plato, is that with every plan of action, you have to be able to adapt to any tide and accept all unexpected currents," Nori says. "The first wave might not be the best, so you have to carefully design a master *strategy* and always be willing to readjust your execution of the specific knowledge gained."

"That is a magnificent answer, my sea turtle friend!" Plato responds. "Do not confuse intelligence with self-awareness. All creatures are brilliant in their own unique way. We as a species have developed our brain for communication, echolocation and complex social networks amongst ourselves. For a creature that has a less complex cognitive ability, you are a wise young one.

"You are not like the rest of the creatures we have met who use their brain, particularly the humans. You see, we live in a beautiful world where land and sea will always cross paths."

"Land always adapts and changes to the wants of mankind, but the sea is untamable," Aristotle explains. "It is dominated by those who can develop and evolve internally, rather than externally. Those who live on land are more concerned about having than being. However, they are also amazing executives of time, and great fun to swim with!"

"Executives of time?" Nori says, pondering this new term.

"Yes!" Socrates adds to his brother's thought frequency. "Time is the only luxury we all share, so the ability to *Implement* your dreams is determined by the wise use of your time. Have no fear my friend, you are a sea turtle who executes travel with respect to time. For those who do not travel, never get to see the world because they TH!NK they don't have the time."

"That is because they do not make the time. They say *I can't* instead of asking **how can I** and then following it with an **I WILL** affirmation," Nori says, indicating his understanding of the bottlenose dolphins lesson.

"Those who do not make the time to follow their passions, waste time in their small, comfortable microhabitat. Instead they should get uncomfortable. Explore and increase their awareness in our ultimate habitat. The more room to live, the more room to grow. You as a sea turtle know this!" Plato affirms, mimicking his brothers' behavior in synergy.

"Where does your path take you next, my friend?" Aristotle asks the green sea turtle.

"I am on a journey to see the wise Great Jonathan, the oldest living turtle, on the island of Saint Helena. Can you show me the way?"

"Ah yes, a true leader learns the way, then shows the way! You are right now in the Pacific Ocean. You have to go to the Atlantic Ocean. There are two logical paths. One requires you to go through the cold waters of Argentina. The second is the one traveled the least, through the muddy sweet waters of the Panama Canal. Whichever you choose shall not be easy."

"The Panama Canal," Nori mused. "That is the way I shall continue on my path seeking Jonathan, the great giant tortoise."

Socrates chuckles and echoes, "That's the spirit, my determined little friend! On your journey for **K**nowledge, don't forget—unless it is applied, it is entirely useless potential."

Plato follows with the statement, "Until it is applied **S**trategically, you will not reach your ultimate goal!"

Aristotle finishes the conversation with, "Only when you **I**mplement your plans of action, shall you achieve your goal using the knowledge gained through your experiences."

The three dolphins swim off together in parallel formation, in the opposite of the direction in which Nori is traveling.

Alone again, he is fascinated by the new insights. Feeling great, he is well on his way to continuing the journey he began all those years ago in Hawaii. His sea turtle mindset has served him well, and his courage has grown as he's challenged himself with the obstacles that have come his way.

As a baby turtle, he did not quit! Even when the tides were against him, pulling him back to shore, forcing him to start from scratch again. All he knew was that as long as he just kept on swimming, one flipper at a time, he would arrive. Nori kept his head sticking out, and once he reached his first destination, he was able to see even further. The sea turtle mindset is about consistency and perseverance. The sea turtle does whatever it takes to succeed.

Thus, Nori begins to swim once again, following the instructions given to him by his latest mentors, the dolphins. He is determined to swim the Central American coastline until he reaches the sweet waters of the Panama Canal.

Yes, he tells himself as he swims, a sea turtle does whatever it takes to succeed.

Notes

_____

_____

_____

_____

_____

_____

_____

_____

(Words of wisdom…One of America's leading universities discovered that people exposed to new information one time retains only about 2% of it two weeks later. So reading and writing will be at least two exposures!)

#SeaTurtleMindset

YouTube Chapter Video
http://bit.ly/SeaTurtleMindsetChapter6

CHAPTER 5

Focus

"Focus On One Task Instead Of Multitasking"

Zealously Nori found himself in zealous pursuit of the wisdom of the Great Jonathan from Saint Helena. It was the eighth night since he had met his dolphin friends, and he had not taken rest. The excitement would not let him sleep. He was only making quick stops for seaweed to re-energize himself, and off he'd go swimming again.

Determined to reach the Panama Canal as soon as possible, he is exhausted from his efforts. But this does not stop the sea turtle. Occasionally rising to the surface, he takes deep breaths of the fresh sea salt air. The stars above are his guides, and as the night breeze hits his beak, it is all the prodding he needs to continue on his route.

During one of his breaks from swimming, Nori admires the sight of the glowing jellyfish around him. He observes how the motion of squeezing their bodies in order to push water from beneath them propels the jellyfish forward. They elegantly dance with the wave current, glowing and flickering their inner lights.

All of a sudden, Nori feels the same presence he felt the day he fought off the tiger shark. In high alert, Nori takes another deep breath and plunges deep into the sea, where the pressure is intense.

Having practiced this ability with Maximus, he avoids any animal that cannot handle that degree of pressure on their body.

"Sea turtles usually travel during the day. They can't see well at night," a disembodied voice says from the deep blue abyss.

"I have a burning desire to seek wisdom from the wisest. I, Nori, make myself do what I choose to do, whether I feel like it or not. I believe I can and I will succeed," he responds defiantly as he looks around in the dark blue waters.

"Are you not afraid of the unknown?" the voice replies.

"I replace the fear with curiosity. The unknown is just another opportunity to become great."

"Well then, Nori, I am Zamerat the Octopus, and I must say: you are a very courageous sea turtle."

"It is great to meet you, Zamerat!" Nori enthusiastically responds, still trying to find him with his eyes. "So, what are you exactly? I will not stay until the sun rises to see for myself."

"Well, as an octopus, I have eight tentacles arms. Unlike your four flippers, my eight limbs have suction cups that even if I lose, I can re-grow with no permanent damage."

"No permanent damage you say? That is very fascinating! Tell me, Zamerat, having all those arms, you must be very skillful with handling multiple tasks at once, right?" Nori questions the octopus.

"On the contrary, my friend, yes I can say my ability to multitask is ideal, but the most valuable attribute I have is my ability to *FOCUS*."

"Please explain," Nori says, "because I have struggled from time to time executing multiple tasks all at once."

"Certainly," Zamerat replies. "Having eight arms ,I have the ability to hold rocks, defend myself, swim, and also hold my food. But why would I stress myself with all of these obstacles at the same time? Instead of accomplishing eight tasks with twelve percent quality effort, I prefer accomplishing one task with one-hundred percent quality effort."

"So, what you're saying is that multitasking is inefficient in quality, and focus is key for optimal quality?" Nori responds, gaining a sudden realization.

"Ahh, you learn fast—correct! Similar to how I am able to focus my whole body into fitting within impossible-sized cracks, the brain can do the same when focused on a single task."

"Multitasking should be avoided, then!" Nori declares. "Tell me, Zamerat: how are you able to fit your body into the smallest crack?"

"First, I visualize the goal already accomplished, before even focusing my mind on the actual task. Second, I prepare myself mentally for any failures that may come to pass, because in anything you do, you have to fail forward to have a successful outcome. For example, even when I fail to squeeze myself through a crack, I've simply discovered one way that doesn't work. I visualize again using a different method until I fit my body through."

"Visualize?" the sea turtle ponders as he is at a standstill in the open waters.

"Yes, visualization is the most powerful tool that the mind has. It is powered by your ability of imagination. For example, your goal is to reach the wisest turtle. Simply imagine yourself in front of his presence already." Zamerat explains. He then takes form by camouflage with the jellyfish around, all eight tentacles glowing a neon blue from the suction cups and orange-red body of the octopus.

"I see!" Nori gasps, fascinated by the new ability he's learned, as well as by seeing an octopus for the first time.

"*Envision, Envision, Envision!* Only that which is planted first in the mind can become a fact in the world." Zamerat declares. With a whirl of his body , he swims swiftly around Nori.

"I am grateful for your wisdom, Zamerat. I hope we shall meet again shortly," Nori says, continuing to swim to his destination.

"Visualize, my friend," the octopus calls after him, "and just as knowledge is only potential power, so it is nothing without implementation! One swish of a flipper is all it takes to execute! Remember to focus on one task!"

Nori continues to swim boldly into the night. Time is not of his concern. Instead, he is glad to be living in the moment.

Nori realizes now that any being is always just seconds away from capturing a wonderful experience. Why, he just met an octopus! Instead of focusing on the past and wasting your time, or focusing so fully on what's to come that you miss the present beauty, just focus on living in the moment, and it all becomes an adventure. You never know when you will create a memory that lasts a lifetime. Embrace every turtle second!

As he swims, Nori begins to use the tool offered to him by Zamerat. He visualizes the giant tortoise. He lets go of worrying about how he will find him on Saint Helena, nor what questions he will ask. He simply envisions his presence.

As dawn is far from approaching, Nori still is unable to see the shore, but his burning desire to reach his destination is intensifying with every stroke of his fins. He can picture it now, how he will feel in the presence of the Great Jonathan.

And so he paddles on. And on. And on.

Notes

_____

_____

_____

_____

_____

_____

_____

_____

_____

(Words of wisdom...One of America's leading universities discovered that people exposed to the same information on six consecutive days they will remember 62% of it two weeks later!)

#SeaTurtleMindset

YouTube Chapter Video
http://bit.ly/SeaTurtleMindsetChapter5

CHAPTER 4

"Just Be A Happy Sea Turtle"

Captivated by the lessons he has learned along the way, Nori lays on his shell, floating on the surface of the Pacific. It is a calm night in the infinite waters of the ocean, and the sky is an endless sea of stars. As he slowly floats on the ocean waves, Nori drifts into a deep sleep and begins to dream about meeting Jonathan the giant tortoise. In his dream, Nori has arrived on the island of Saint Helena and is looking for the direction of his mentor.

Morning arrives, and the sun is shining right over the East horizon. Nori wakes up to a tingling sensation in his shell. He realizes he is being cleaned by small fishes of yellow, blue and black. Nori smiles. He must be arriving at a coral reef! He takes a deep breath, flips over, and dives into the endless colors of the reef.

Schools of different fishes swim passed him, a group of them still cleaning his shell and making it shine. From a quick flash of the tail, he spots another sea turtle. It's the perfect opportunity to ask for directions to the Panama Canal.

"Excuse me, excuse me! I am looking for the Panama Canal. Would you be able to show me the way," Nori asks politely of his fellow sea turtle.

"Well, of course I can!" says the sea turtle in a sweet and gentle voice.

Nori had never met a female sea turtle, and he is stunned by her beautiful lime green shell and log shaped head.

"Mmmm...ma...ma...my name is Nori," he stammers. "I'm a green sea turtle on a mission to seek and spread the wisdom of the oldest turtle alive."

She laughs at his nervous introduction.

"My name is Sofia. I'm a loggerhead sea turtle on a mission to find food!" As Sofia swims closer to Nori, she notices the nasty scar on his left back flipper and gasps, "What happened to your flipper?"

"A few months ago, I was feeding on seaweed, and a tiger shark surprised me with a nice bite on my flipper. It's okay—I am sure he has a memory of me on his fins," he confidently answers.

"Impressive—fighting off a shark! Well, you are in luck, my friend. I am actually on my way to the exact same beach near the canal where I hatched, but this time I'm going to lay my own eggs." She begins to swim again with Nori by her side.

"I have not returned home since I left on my journey," Nori explains, remembering the soft sand of Hawaii.

"When you do go back," Sofia tells him as she swims around him swiftly, "no matter how far you travel, internally you will always know how to go home.

When you decide to go back, it's the happiest feeling ever."

"Happiness is always inside of you," Nori tells her. "You must practice it so that it becomes a mental habit and attitude that you learn to use in the present. When my attitude changes because of certain circumstances, I simply go to my happy place and I dream about the beach, and it always makes me happy." As he shares these thoughts with Sofia, Nori can almost feel the sand under his flippers.

"I could not agree with you more, Nori," Sofia replies. "On my journey, I have learned that happiness is not given to you. The decision to be happy is yours to make. No single thing will make you happy until you choose to be happy. Happiness comes from within, not from without."

They swim through a sunken shipwreck, getting closer to the shores of Panama.

"The only thing that is truly important is how we control our emotions and how we feel inside, not what others perceive on the outside," Nori says. "The power of emotions is what manifests our true happiness. If you are going to be happy, just be happy no matter what is happening! There is no need to swim in your sorrows, let them fade away like the tides on the beach."

"Feelings are like the waves Nori, we can't stop them from coming, but we can decide which ones to surf.

We are just two happy turtles swimming to the beach! I love it!" Sofia exclaims. "This is my first time laying eggs. I am so excited!!"

"Those little baby sea turtles are coming into a world of abundance," Nori says, recalling his own entrance into the world. "I remember when I hatched, all I wanted to do was explore!"

"It fascinates me that as soon we sea turtles hatch from our eggs, we make the DECISION to explore and head straight to the ocean," Sofia says. "All together without hesitation, we find our way because indecision means that the seagulls will get you and fly away with your dreams. We look for the brightest light in the sky, and aim towards the moon. Some of us don't even get the chance to break our eggs." Sofia pauses and swims to the surface. "There it is, my friend, the Panama canal! It won't be easy swimming through it. There are all different kinds of creatures in those waters, and it's also not usual for a sea turtle to take this path."

"I understand your concern, but I am not your average sea turtle, Sofia," Nori says with a wink. "Thank you for the insight you have given me. We shall meet again!" Nori dives back down and begins to swim in his own direction. Sofia calls after him.

"Before you go, do you mind me asking: what are you looking for on the other side of the Panama Canal?"

"I am propelling through to reach the Atlantic Ocean, where I can swim happily and become richer than I already am!" Nori calls back.

"Rich?" Sofia replies, confused by his answer

"Yes, we all deserve to be rich in the purest sense. The riches of life are what make life worth living!"

"How do I become rich?" Sofia asks, very curious about this new insight.

Nori laughs pleasantly.

"Sofia, you already are rich. Nevertheless, the eleven riches of life that I have learned thus far first begin with our love of travel. As we travel the world, our mind is enriched with different perspectives and cultures. (1) "We gain a positive mental attitude when we learn to appreciate what we have instead of longing for what we don't.

"Being optimistic keeps you healthy. Which leads to the second richness of life: having sound physical health. All the swimming around the world causes you to be buoyant with life. (2)

"Our conversation on happiness was really about the third richness. This helps us be harmonious in all relationships, including our own with ourselves. (3)

"Once we begin using these riches we are led to the fourth freedom. Our ability to travel gives us physical and mental freedom from limitations and fears.(4)

"The fifth richness is love. You have been radiating love since the moment I met you. Love is all around, and to engage in the labour of love makes you rich. (5)

"The sixth richness is having certainty and trust, which we have demonstrated by swimming straight into the ocean as hatchlings. Taking on the world demonstrates faith. (6)

"The seventh is hope of mastery in goals and dreams. You are about to fulfill one of your goals soon on the beach by becoming a mother. (7)

"When those eggs hatch, you will share all of your experiences when you meet your children in the ocean. The willingness to share one's blessings with others makes you rich. The act of giving is when you truly receive riches. (8)

"Having an open mind to all subjects and all creatures is being rich. (9) This increases your self-awareness and allows you to be present. Some sea turtles swim to simply exist, while others are swimming to be alive.

"To be rich is to have complete self-discipline. (10) This will be difficult in the beginning. It won't be easy, but the results from self-discipline will be worth the sweat equity.

"Lastly, the wisdom to understand others makes you truly rich. (11) Being understood is good, but understanding others makes you great!"

Nori finishes his list with a huge smile.

"Thank you for sharing that, Nori! And always remember, life is like the beach—enjoy the waves!!" Sofia shouts to him, her voice full of love and enthusiasm. "Come back to visit and share your wisdom with my hatchlings!"

As he swims towards the canal, Nori recalls his energy and mindset from his very first experience as a baby sea turtle. This sea turtle mindset that catapults Nori into a resourceful state of mind always has one main ingredient. This unique ingredient is found in all sea turtles: it is an intense energy from within.

Dear Reader: To harness this energy, practice your ability to say "I am." You are the main ingredient you need to accomplish anything you set out to do. Your inner sea turtle allows you to take on the impossible. The sea turtle mindset is the attitude of repetition. It is the habit of repetition. Every time you start a new journey or endeavor you are not an expert. You must practice, practice, and practice until it becomes second nature. If we are what we repeatedly do, happiness is then not an act, but a mental habit created by repetition. The same holds true for success, or any virtue we wish to realize in our lives. And so it is true for our little friend Nori as he approaches the Panama Canal. He is about to undertake a feat that is not at all the usual for a sea turtle. But he has been practicing being unusual all his life. And so, he swims on with confidence.

Notes

_____

_____

_____

_____

_____

_____

_____

_____

(Words of wisdom…my hope is that your not concerned on how fast you can read and can "get out" of the book, but instead of how much the book can "get out" of you)

#SeaTurtleMindset

YouTube Chapter Video
.http://bit.ly/SeaTurtleMindsetChapter4

CHAPTER 3

"Action is greater than Reaction"

At the gates of the Panama Canal, Nori has no clue what lies in store on the other side. He has spoken with several sea turtles in the reefs nearby about the journey through the canal. They told him they do not take that path, for it was not the path most would swim. Nevertheless, he understood that you must do what others won't, if you're to have what others can't. If it meant swimming through the uncommon route, so be it.

After several hours of waiting nearby, Nori saw a ship heading toward the gates. He quickly made the decision to follow this ship through the gates and swim alongside. The excitement led emotions to flood his shell.

Emotion is energy in motion and energy flows where attention goes. Every day the ocean produces massive amounts of energy. This energy is always in consistent motion. Energy moves like water; when you block water from its natural flow, it builds up and eventually it breaks the barriers.

By focusing attention on his passion and goals, any sea turtle can overcome obstacles, be they the size of a shrimp or the size of a blue whale. Nori swims with positive emotions because he is just forty-eight miles removed from the Atlantic Ocean.

The gates open, and Nori rushes head first before the boat, not realizing that when the gates open, it causes a rush of water back into the ocean. Nori spins and tumbles backwards and hits the ocean floor.

He rebalances himself and he tries again. This time he swims behind the ship, keeping at a good distance so that he does not tailgate the currents. He passes the first set of gates and TH!NKS it's a straight shot to the Atlantic. He swims past the cargo ship and discovers a second pair of gates.

Confused, he swims to see if there is another way around the gates, but there are four walls surrounding him. He is certain that there is a way to get out of this box, the ocean is too tremendous in size to not be able to TH!NK outside the box. The only way through, however, is when the gates open. Nori resolves not to get frustrated. Instead, he explores his surroundings.

As his awareness of his environment increases, he starts to notice that the water begins to rise. Time passes by, the water halts from rising, and the gates begin to open. Learning from his previous experience, he waits until they are fully open to pick up speed. After swimming through, yet another gate blocks his path. He remains patient once again, certain that it will open in time. Moments later, these large chamber gates are indeed opened to a new world.

As he passes through the gates, Nori realizes that he has finally entered the Panama Canal. The water has completely changed in flavor; it is no longer salty, but instead sweet. The color has also changed into a muddy brown very different from the Pacific Ocean.

He swims up to a fork in the river. He looks right, and then he looks left. The river splits in two. Puzzled, he decides to go onto land. He is startled by the creature he encounters.

It is crouched oddly, with a hairy body, black patches on his head, a white face, and black hairy hands and feet. It is eating a yellow cylindrical food which Nori has never seen.

"Hello there!" Nori calls up to the creature. "What sort of animal are you?"

"I'm a monkey, of course!" the creature laughs.

"Where can I find myself some food, my monkey friend?" Nori asks as his stomach growls.

"Up the tree you must go!" the monkey laughs, peeling its food with its teeth. It points at a tree. Then it looks at Nori's flippers and laughs again.

Nori simply smiles at the monkey, and in a kind tone, he says, "Young one, I have something for you."

The young monkey's eyes widen. "What is it?" he asks very curiously. He approaches, coming closer and closer to the edge of the water.

"Treat others the same way you want to be treated," Nori says, sharing the golden rule.

!SPLASH! Jaws come right out the water and snap at the monkey. The young one drops its food and flees into the jungle.

Alarmed, Nori looks around. He holds his fear at bay and observes the creature with the teeth. He scolds it:

"That was very uncalled for you, you, you..." He tries to figure out what kind of beast he is staring at. It has an overbite, a huge green nose, and big yellow teeth.

"Crocodile" the beast proudly ends his sentence "A long time ago I took a bite of a sea turtle, but I lost several teeth. Monkeys are more soft, tasty and easier to chew" the crocodile responds with a scratchy old voice.
"What river path do I take to the Atlantic ocean? I am determined to reach my destination" Nori replied with no hesitation, adjusting himself on the muddy terrain.

"That is the right mindset, a sea turtle with determination and purpose! Very well, my name is Newton. I have lived in these rivers for fifty-five years. Take the left river path towards the North West and you will enter Lake Gatun. You won't miss the canal gates to the Atlantic."

"Thank you for the guidance, Newton. Are all crocodiles this helpful?"

Newton groans, then begins to laugh. His body vibrates as he laughs, causing the water to dance upon his scaly back. The ripple from his laughter causes the water to look and sound like pebbles falling into a pond. "A long time ago," Newton tells Nori, "I realized that for every action that I take, there is always an opposite reaction that happens. Not every crocodile you meet has taken a bite of a hard shell like yours. My advice is to consistently take action on those vibrations of the body, instead of reacting against them."

"What vibrations do you speak of Newton?"

"Over the years living in the canal, I have been observant of my surroundings. I have found that all creatures in this life go through emotions, also referred to as feelings. These feelings are actually different forms of vibration that the body experiences. From these vibrations, you can also determine what you attract into your life. For example, your feelings of enthusiasm and joy will attract the results of success. If you are feeling sad or fearful, your body's vibration is at the same frequency of failure and downfall. There are positive and negative emotions—vibrations, if you will—that correspond with positive and negative results."

"My goodness, you're a knowledgable beast!" Nori exclaims. "Crocodiles must be quite evolved— you're both helpful and wise. Let me see if I understand: you're saying I should learn to become aware of the vibrations I experience? By doing so, I keep myself in check and protect my thoughts in the same way my shell protects my body?"

"Exactly!" Newton affirms. "And as we've established, that shell of yours is some hefty protection. Stronger than crocodile teeth."

"Thank goodness for that, and thank you for the advice," Nori replies. He reaches for the food the monkey dropped and gets back into the water. "By the way," he asks Newton as he takes a bite, "what is this thing the monkey was eating. It's pretty good."

"It's a banana," Newton says without enthusiasm. "Monkeys taste much better."

Nori laughs and shakes his head.

"So long, Newton. Thank you for the help."

"My pleasure," Newton says. "And remember: Do not allow outward events and other animals to dictate how you should feel, or even how you should react. Purge your mind of worry, fear, and plain old metal debris. This will allow you to take the time to reflect, plan, and dream. Have a great journey, my sea turtle friend!" Newton slowly drifts back into the river, his eyes popping out at the surface for one second before he disappears fully into the muddy waters.

Energy is everywhere around the sea turtle, Nori realizes. It is vital that his thought patterns match the vibration of the energy around him. The vibrations caused by the body create the energy that corresponds to the frequency, and this affects the attraction that will manifest.

Feelings or emotions are cultivated from the heart. The mind and the heart are powerful tools for creation. They work best when congruent with the body. Everything Newton said makes sense. It resonates with Nori's own experience of life.

As he continues to swim toward the lake, Nori is mindful of the nature around him. The sea turtle mindset acknowledges that the bottom of the river is like the past: it is muck that has been settled. If you choose to swim down through the muck, it causes your vision to be blurred. Nori understands that you have to let the muck settle at the bottom, and let go of the idea of swimming through it. Choose to swim above in the present, and your vision of the future will always be clear.

Nori is enjoying his swim in new waters, and he finally reaches the Gatun Canal gates, catching right back up with the cargo ship he was tailgating.

These gates are the same as the first gates, with one big difference. On the other side lies the Atlantic Ocean. Another sea of mysteries, new adventures to uncover, and who knows what creatures Nori might encounter?

The unknown is not something that holds Nori back. In fact, his eagerness to try out new things for the very first time is one of his motivations.

Ah—motivation! Isn't that one of the words his mother used? Nori thinks back fondly. He knows now what that means.

Nothing can hold back a sea turtle mindset. Nori would be more disappointed by the things he did not do than by the things he did do. And so he keeps moving onward, into a new ocean.

Notes

_____

_____

_____

_____

_____

_____

_____

_____

(Words of wisdom… Take action on what you learned, learning without implementing is like never learning in the first place.)

#SeaTurtleMindset

YouTube Chapter Video
http://bit.ly/SeaTurtleMindsetChapter3

CHAPTER 2

IMAGINATION

"Imagination Is Key For Lifestyle Creation"

Nori swims successfully through the canal and travels for several months down the South American coastline. On his journey, he meets several sea turtles from all different countries: Colombia, Venezuela, Guyana, Suriname, French Guiana, and Brazil.

Nori learns a key truth: as you travel the world, you enrich and expand your mind. Once your mind expands, it can't contract to its original state. You are able to see the world with a different perspective. The perspectives of the different kinds of sea turtles Nori meets along the way teach him many things. To travel is to grow from within, and it is the reason sea turtles have a wanderlust.

Nori has been captivated by the different coral reefs he's experienced, the different sea creatures he has met along his journey. His travels expanded his mind to higher degrees of consciousness, and that allows him to communicate excellently with other animals. He knows that everyone he meets is valuable, and he treats them as such. Everyone you meet knows something you don't know—and vice versa. This is a lesson Nori holds in his heart.

It is a beautiful day to be in the ocean, the sky is clear, the water is turquoise with waves crashing against the shore. The white foam collects at the water's edge, and the soft sand runs back into the ocean. As Nori takes rest, he sees a black dolphin near the shoreline. This dolphin is different from his friends. This one is much larger in size, and from its mouth all the way up to its belly, it is white. Around the eyes are large white spots, and it has a large round nose. As Nori dives in the ocean, he is curious to find out more about this black-and-white dolphin.

"Hello there!!" Nori calls out as he approaches the black dolphin. It is flipping in the air, making a huge splash. All of a sudden, Nori notices a shark- like fin approaching fast. His natural instinct is to dive deep.

"Hello Mr. Sea Turtle, How can I be of assistance?" the black dolphin meets him underwater with a polite manner.

"Why are you different from the grey dolphins I met?" Nori asked curiously. He swims around, admiring this dolphin's uniqueness.

The dolphin bursts into laughter. "No wonder you are not afraid of me! I am a Killer Whale. Not a dolphin, exactly, though I'm a relative of the dolphin family. My friends call me Albert the Orca."

"To overcome fear is only the beginning of wisdom," Nori says, "It is a pleasure to meet you, Albert. My name is Nori, the wise sea turtle on a quest to become wiser. Tell me my friend, what do you value the most? What do you TH!INK is your most important quality?""

"My imagination" Albert responds without a second to spare.

"Why is that?" Nori fascinated by his prompt reply

"The ability to TH!NK and imagine is our ultimate tool to get what we want. Imagination helps create our world that we live in: mentally first, and then physically. From the within comes the without. When you consistently imagine the world you want, it will attract its physical counterpart." Albert replies, somewhat nonchalantly.

"How does the imagination work?" Nori asks, completely engaged in this conversation.

"Our mind collects all our experiences, insights, lessons, emotions, and thoughts and stirs them up into one picture. These are our perspectives of life. Imagination allows us to pick and choose the ones we believe in. It also helps us by modeling other perspectives, so we can make a newly imagined picture.

"The reason I value imagination is because you can literally create your world as you speak and as you TH!NK. What you consistently TH!NK about in your imaginary world, well—this invisible part of your life manifests the visible. Your conscious imagination becomes your subconscious nature.

"TH!NK about it: the invisible is infinite, while the visible is limited, and is only merely a representation of the invisible. See, there is always more invisible than visible. There is more imagination than actualization. Imagination is infinite."

"What do you mean by 'modeling?'" Nori asks, curious.

"Ah, yes—modeling. When we simulate with our mind, that cuts the learning curve. We do not have to go through the actual trial and error. We can learn from the mistakes of others. *Model* the good habits and avoid the bad habits. Here is an example: you see a turtle eating with a large school of fish, and typically there are humans fishing with nets around large schools of fish. You then see the turtle getting tangled up in the fishnets. The next time you see a school of fish feeding, are you going to join them for lunch?"

"Certainly not!" Nori exclaims. "Aha! I see what you mean by learning from the mistakes of others. And you can also model the success of others as well. So, *Imagination* allows you to see it before it actually happens?"

"Is that question or a statement?" Albert replies, and he and Nori exchange a smile. "Either way, yes, you are correct." The orca then adds, "Imagination is more important than information. Information is limited to what we already know and understand. But imagination embraces the infinite world we live in— all that we don't know, and all there is to discover still."

"I have another question for you: How do you activate this imagination?" Nori asks. His intense curiosity has been piqued. He wants to know how to activate his own natural ability of imagination.

"Simply close your eyes and dream. TH!NK of whatever your heart desires. Stay true to yourself and hold that imagination vividly in your mind," Albert explains to his wise little friend as he swims to the surface and executes a magnificent back flip. The elegance of his form as his whole body leaps from the water, his anchor shape tail following the splash at the end—all this captivates Nori.

"That is amazing. The world is a canvas for the imagination and creativity. Albert, can you share with me the direction to the island of Saint Helena. I know it is located in the Atlantic."

"You are in luck my friend!" the orca replies. "You are currently in my residence of Salvador, Brazil. All you have to do is literally swim straight to the East. Even when the tides pulls you off the shortest distance from your course, have perseverance and keep swimming straight."

"I really appreciate the insight you have given to me today, Albert," Nori says sincerely. "I ask questions of everyone I meet because everyone has something of value to teach, and everyone knows something I don't."

"To maintain a highly active imagination, don't be afraid to take the lid of your mind and daydream!

Goodbye, my friend, and good luck," Albert the orca shouts.

Nori watches his new friend swim away. He sets his course, thinking about how he is now a couple thousand miles closer to his mentor, the Great Jonathan.

He realizes his imagination has most definitely been activated. It is, in fact, swimming wild!

Notes

_____

_____

_____

_____

_____

_____

_____

_____

_____

(Words of wisdom... Logic will get you from A to B. Imagination will take you everywhere -Albert Einstein)

#SeaTurtleMindset

YouTube Chapter Video
http://bit.ly/SeaTurtleMindsetChapter2

CHAPTER 1

"TH!NK & DO"

The sky is rolling in some dark clouds from the West. Nori is surrounded by the silence of the sun rays and the aquatic noise underneath him. Practicing taking deep breaths is one of his healthy habits. His sea turtle imagination is swimming faster than he actually is.

The day after meeting Albert, he slept through the morning and woke up mid-afternoon. He quickly realized that sleeping is essential to regaining energy —and he needs energy to make those dreams come true! So he decided: each day he would experiment in his ocean laboratory and learn how many hours of sleep made him feel amazing after waking up, and how many hours made him feel sluggish after waking up. On the sixty-sixth day, his internal alarm clock changed into his new habit of sleeping.

Sixty-six days have passed since his encounter with Albert the Orca. Ever since then, Nori's mind has completely changed old habits into new habits. One of the habits he changed within this time frame was relying on his TH!NKING strengths rather than his weaknesses.

All turtles share the ability to th!nk, but not all turtles th!nk alike. Everyone th!nks with their own unique structured brain. In fact as Nori traveled, he discovered that there are seven types of th!nking sea turtles have.

All sea turtles have a dominant th!nking abilities followed by less dominant th!nking potential. Each of the seven turtles th!nking is responsible for certain traits and characteristics. Knowing how you th!nk will enable you to comprehend more knowledge, more connections will form in your mind, and you will be able to act with wisdom instead of reacting like a fool.

There are seven types of sea turtles in the world, who all have a dominant th!nking ability and share each way of th!nking in their own unique combination :

Green Sea Turtles: Often have high intrapersonal intelligence which means they like to look inward for answers. Green Sea Turtles seek understanding and are introspective. They are aware of their emotions, motivations, and beliefs. This includes a deep understanding of themselves, their limiting beliefs and goals. Intrapersonal communication stays within the sea turtle's mind which is also the basis of all other communication. The understanding of and response of what we hear and learn depends on this type of th!nking. Green sea turtles also understand the importance of regulating their self talk from negative to positive.

Leatherback Sea Turtles: Often are great at building momentum by staying active and having body awareness. Would rather touch physically than just look. Always ready to dive deep into the ocean and love movement. They feel out the environment by exploring and learn by doing. Leatherback turtles use the body to express ideas and they love speed. They excel interacting with one's environment and gaining concrete experiences.

Loggerhead Sea Turtles: Use visual intelligence to th!nk. They are very aware of their surroundings and are excellent at remembering places and images. They have a great sense of direction. They love to learn visually and organize ideas spatially. Always th!nking in images and pictures and "seeing" things in one's mind. They learn best when they are able to visualize what they want to happen.

Hawksbill Sea Turtles: Use more of their linguistic intelligence to th!nk. They love and are talented with words. They have a great ability to teach and explain things to others. Sometimes use fancy words and always quoted others who they have learned from. They excel in listening to spoken word.

Kemp's Ridley Sea Turtles: Use their logical intelligence. They typically are abstract th!nkers and are attracted to logic and reasoning. They are great with investigations and discovering how things work and why. They learn best by logic and solving problems for complete comprehension.

Olive Ridley Sea Turtles: Use interpersonal intelligence which makes them good with other sea turtles and thrive in social interactions at coral reefs. They are good at understanding, reading and empathize with other sea creatures. They are good at working with others and have many friends. They learn best through interaction and dialogue. They love to collaborate and are cooperatively.

Flatback Sea Turtles: Have a musical intelligence which means they love the songs of the ocean. The sounds that come from all parts, from deep silence to crowded coral reefs with all life. Flatback sea turtles notice and enjoy different sounds. They learn through songs, rhythms, patterns and musical expression. Often are found singing, whistling and using their shells as drums.

Nori's interaction with different sea turtles gave him a clear understanding that everyone operates through a combination of these multiple intelligences and this is how all turtles th!nk differently, all sea turtles are unique. Knowing your own combination will help you identify what kind of sea turtle you are. By knowing how you th!nk, you will be able to focus more on your strengths and worry less on your *complementary* weaknesses.

Nori is a strong logical th!nker but living with Maximus the leatherback sea turtle also learned by doing, diving right into life's greatest experiences and adversities. So he uses both intelligences when th!nking and making decisions. After the sequence of thoughts he uses his visual intelligence by visualizing his dreams of what he wants to accomplish.

In his dreams, he would already be in the presence of his wise mentor, but when he would wake up, he would have no idea how he was going to do the "impossible". When he would th!nk of the word "impossible" he would rewire his mind by saying "*Im-possible* to do anything I set my mind to do."

It has been a long time since he wobbled upland, the last time he was a baby sea turtle, now fully grown he knew the challenge that awaits at the island of Saint Helena. He arrives mentally prepared.

The rain begins to pour on Nori's shell, the storm catching up with him. You never know when a storm is coming, Nori thinks—it's best just to be ready to embrace them. There are some things you can only learn by going through storms.

As the darkness of the clouds blocks the sun, thunder and lightning break the silence of the ocean. Waves grow to tremendous size, and Nori is struggling to swim straight on the surface. So he takes a deep breath and swims under. While chaos is above him, he finds the calmness beneath the surface of the ocean.

The lightning illuminates the water, trailing cracking thunder that causes vibrations in the water around Nori. The winds gusting at the surface of the ocean form into one hundred foot waves. Beneath the water, it is still hard for Nori to swim. He is wrestling against Mother Nature to stay on track and not get tossed up in the storm.

When he would become weak, he would just remember that storms do not last forever. They can frighten you, they can even vibrate you to your core. But it never lasts forever. The down pour turns to a soft drizzle and the thunder dies. The gust of winds turn into a soft whisper and the dark clouds disappear. A moment later the sun begins to peek out, the waves go all silent and still.

And so it happens for Nori this time. The sea turtle has a gentle peace of mind, like the first time he went into the ocean. The storm passes, and he rises to the surface.

As Nori goes up for another breath of air, the clouds roll away on the horizon. The sound of seagulls in the distance offers a sign of land. This fuels Nori with energy to swim harder and faster. The motivation that kept him on a consistent path now leaves him with no doubt in his mind that this is the island where he will find the oldest living turtle in the world. As the shoreline becomes more visible, the island shows its volcanic qualities, reminding Nori of Hawaii.

As he draws closer to shore, he begins to have urges to slow down. His journey has exhausted him, and the storm has taken a lot of his energy. Even though he overcame the distractions along the way, seeing the shoreline is only the beginning. Slowing down once you see the prize is where most sea turtles fail. Instead of slowing down, Nori puts more urgency into his swimming.

At last Nori feels the solid shoreline under his flippers. His first steps onto wet sand could suck him back into the ocean if he allows it. As he keeps wobbling along, the wet solid ground quickly turns into soft, hot sand.

As the sun is setting, he decides to rest his mind for the night. After overcoming the storm, he does not remember how he made it through or how he managed to stay on track. He is not even sure if the storm was really over or if had just begun. But one thing was certain, he knew: when you come out of the storm, you won't be the same sea turtle who swam into it.

That's what storms do, they change you.

The sound of the waves gently crashing on the sand—nature's lullaby—soon sends Nori drifting into refreshing sleep.

Notes

_____

_____

_____

_____

_____

_____

_____

_____

Words of wisdom… Storms come in many different forms, embrace and trust the process. Storms truly do make you stronger!

#SeaTurtleMindset

YouTube Chapter Video
.http://bit.ly/SeaTurtleMindsetChapter1

CHAPTER 0

Wisdom Teacher

"You're a Sea Turtle, Aren't You?"

Nori awakes before the sunrise and starts to wobble upland. He has forgotten what the ground felt like, but he does remember what Elder Tortuga told him when he was a baby sea turtle: "A journey of a thousand miles starts with one flipper."

He wobbles upland, struggling with each increment, dragging his body on rocks and sea shell terrain. He scratches the skin under his flippers, and he feels them becoming dry under the sun.

As he approached the main road, a seagull asked "Aren't you a sea turtle? Sea turtles CAN"T walk on land!".

Nori turns around and says, "Can't they? WATCH ME!"

Seagulls, Nori knows, are like negative thoughts or negative opinions, *you feed one what it wants, and a flock will come.* Do not feed the seagulls what they want and stay positive on your path, Nori tells himself! To get what you want, the sea turtle understands you have to put in the work. You will get what you want only when you deserve it. You won't climb a mountain by staring at it.

Persistently, the seagull continues to laugh at Nori, and finally lands on his shell and asks, "Okay, Mr. Sea Turtle who can,—where are you going?"

"I'm here to meet Jonathan, the great tortoise. Do you know the direction I should take?"

"Oh, Jonathan? Everybody knows Jonathan! You are on the right path, Just keep on this path and you will find the plantation where he lives with humans!" the seagull shouts as he flaps away.

On the other side of the road is Jonathan himself, walking on the same path. The night of the storm, the gusts caused the gates to open. His high sense of hearing allowed him to hear the gates of the plantation squeak back and forth before sunrise. He had never ventured away from his home, but he had the intuition to walk in that direction that morning. Being blind, it was difficult for Jonathan to find his way around, but he would keep his beak to the ground and smelled the monkey ears to stay off the main road.

After walking half the night, Jonathan grew tired and laid on a patch of his favorite monkey ear herbs. Jonathan was under the shade of a tree relaxing, as the morning turned into afternoon. Nori, now, is just a few hundred feet away, with no clue that his dream of meeting the wisest and oldest turtle was mere moments from coming true.

Relentless on the volcanically-created path of Saint Helena, Nori continues to drag his turtle body, every wobble harder than the last. As a full grown green sea turtle, Nori is about the size of six-foot tall human and weighs around three hundred and fifty pounds. Humans see him wobbling up the road, but cannot stop him from reaching his goal.

Distractions flash through his mind: what if he does not reach Jonathan? This "what if" mentality was simply another obstacle he'd had to overcome during his journey to seek knowledge. When he had doubt in his mind, he would invert the negative question of what if into a positive one. Instead of saying, "what if I don't?" he would say, "what if I DO!"

Now, though, he is so tired, it is difficult to control those "what ifs." He bats them aside like flies. Nori grows hungrier with every motion of his flippers, hungrier physically and mentally. Then just when he is about to get off the road and settle in a patch of herbs, he sees him.

Jonathan.

He knows it is him. He'd know him from a million miles away. His shell has many scars, relics of millions of untold stories. He is resting under the shade of a tree, tucked into his own world inside his shell. Nori grows very anxious as he wobbles up to the giant turtle.

This is it.

He clears his throat.

"Excuse me my friend, But are you, Jonathan?"

"Yes, I am," the sleepy tortoise replies. "Who are you?"

"I am who I am, Sir. I have come a few thousand miles to seek the wisdom of the oldest turtle alive. My name is Nori."

"Ahh, you are the one I have been seeking." Jonathan says. He sticks his head out and stretches his neck to smell Nori. "You smell salty, young one, tell me—are you a Land Turtle or a Sea Turtle?" He groans and lets loose a peal of laughter.

"I was raised as a land turtle and discovered I had a sea turtle mindset. You have been searching for me?" Nori asks with a laugh in his voice.

"Yes, I have been searching for you. I do not have the same ability as you to travel the world and spread the knowledge I have gained through 184 years. But a sea turtle—a sea turtle could do that for sure!"

"What would you say is the key to living longer?" Nori asks, beginning his interview.

"As I moved from Seychelles to Saint Helena, I learned it is not the most powerful animals that survive, and it's not the most clever animals that survive. It is the one who is most adaptable to change. So don't be a Dodo bird," Jonathan laughs in his old cracking-thunder voice.

"How did you increase your ability to adapt?"

"I became very aware. Self-awareness, I would say, is the second key to living a long life. Before I went blind, I used my sight as vision. The more I saw, the less I would speak. The less I spoke, the more I heard. Now my ability to observe and LISTEN is tremendous."

"Ah, yes!" Nori says, "We don't learn from talking. We learn from listening. When we talk, we only say what we know. But when we listen, we are learning what we don't know. I listen with the goal to understand, rather than the desire to reply." Nori laughs. "Well, except that I just gave you a rather long reply there, didn't I?"

"Ah, very good—you are a great student of increasing consciousness! You are indeed self-aware. Now listen up, for I am going to feed you the eleven seeds of greatness that you shall sow into the minds of thousands."

"I am a little hungry," Nori says, as his stomach growls loudly.

"You see these monkey ears," Jonathan says, "they are my favorite. Eat them, for they are very good for you. Just like how you feed your body daily, you must also feed your mind daily. For when the body and mind are one, they work as one."

As Nori begins to indulge in the delicacy of green monkey ear herbs, Jonathan begins to dole out the mental nourishment that the sea turtle sought.

"Our minds are like gardens, the seeds we plant every day determines our harvest. The seeds are our thoughts attached to emotions. These emotions determine how we feel, which ultimately determines how our days go. Every morning when you arise, remember to cultivate these seeds and continuously plant them in your garden. Throughout the day you shall be watering them. These seeds will create the energy that surrounds you in the ocean.

"If we plant seeds of negative emotions, we will have negative results and effects. To plant the seeds that create a fantastic and zealous life, you must plant the seeds of greatness. A weed plant comes from negativity growing in your garden. This is a warning sign. It means it is time for you to rip these weeds out from their roots so that other plants can grow without stress. Every day, sow the kinds of plants you want to harvest, and extinguish the weeds as soon as you notice them.

"These are the eleven energy seeds you can plant in your garden. If you care for and encourage the growth of these seeds you will hold yourself to a quality of greatness. By putting all your focus on the feelings you want to feel every day, these seeds will create a life that flourishes and fulfills its highest possibility."

1. The seed of LOVE is the most powerful of all. Love is like water. The anger in everyone is like fire which is scorching and dangerous, but it can be put out with love. Being a sea turtle, you love the water. Communication with love excels beyond any other type of reaction. When

someone is enraged or has a temper, if you respond with the state of love, they will change by adopting your loving energy. The fire is put out, and all that is left is love. Life comes from love, so feel and give love daily.

2. Appreciation and gratitude—these energy seeds are two pees in a pod. Appreciation is the acknowledgment and enjoyment of someone or situation. Gratitude is the quality of being thankful. Appreciate the brain that you have for the ability to TH!NK. It is one of the greatest gifts to be grateful for. Nurturing these seeds will harvest an attitude of gratitude.

3. The seed that has lead you on this path to find me was the seed of curiosity. It is the strong desire to know and learn more. As a baby sea turtle, you were most curious. Keep listening to that baby sea turtle in your mind to explore, dream and discover.

4. The enthusiasm seed is my favorite of all. To cultivate this seed, get excited and passionate every day. A sea turtle is only truly great when he acts on his passion. Great enthusiasm in a pursuit of a cause is the result of a zealous harvest.

5. The seed of willpower is determination. The cultivation of this plant will get you all that you ask for. When you seek the energy to overcome obstacles; you shall find the congruent commitment to finish all you set out to do. This

seed produces the fruits of self discipline. It is difficult, but it will be worth it.

6. The answer to your first question of how to live longer was the ability to adapt. The seed of adaptability is the ability to change plans when original plans do not go accordingly. Plans will always change, but decisions don't. Nature is always changing, it is very flexible since it is uncontrollable. We are also like nature. Our minds can change when we change our mindset. To control our minds is to be flexible with the uncontrollable thoughts that are not ours. If we don't adapt and change our th!nking, our minds become uncontrollable and begin to control us.

7. The seventh seed is commitment. Plant this seed and you shall have what you are looking for. You are always committed to something. Be committed to your goals and dreams. Planting these seeds will give you great responsibilities and loyalty. If you are not committed, you're in fact committed to not being committed, and you will constantly harvest nothing but the same seeds of no-commitments.

8. If you plant the seeds above daily, you will certainly have cultivated the seed of trust. This plant produces high levels of self-assurance in one's ability to perform any task. It is having the belief of certainty about the truth. Having faith in yourself to do the impossible. Like walking upland as a sea turtle. This seed builds your

confidence to continue swimming toward your goals.

9. The seed of cheerfulness is one that many do not have. As a sea turtle you naturally have buoyancy. To cultivate this plant more, simply smile. It takes less effort to smile than it does to frown, plus it increases your inner happiness naturally. When turtles notice your happiness and buoyancy in nature they will be happier as a result because they will also feel it. We are all energy and we can feel the energy around us everywhere we go. Others can also feel the energy we bring. So smile when you swim :-)

10. The seed of vitality—as a sea turtle you will always constantly plant this seed. Feeling healthy is a great way to become great. Keep swimming every day. The day you decide to stop swimming is the day you are wasting your energy by doing nothing.

11. The last energy seed to cultivate every day is giving. The seed of giving will empower you, amplify your feelings of fun, freedom, and fulfillment. Only by giving are you able to receive more than you already have. This seed will help you spread joy all around to those you meet.

"These seeds I have planted in you now, Nori, and you are to give them back to the world. When you learn something, you practice it. After you practice it, you teach it. Remember: teach only what you practice, and that has been my contribution to you. Namaste, all-wise Nori." Jonathan bows his head to him.

"Thank you, Jonathan. Power is gained by sharing knowledge, not keeping it for yourself," Nori replies with appreciation.

"Everything you're looking for is already inside you, you just have to TH!NK about it. Remember: knowledge is potential power, execution of it is vital. A sea turtle's purpose is to travel and become wise. A sea turtle mind is one that creates a magnificent obsession for life's riches.

"Always remember every failure begins with the seed of an equivalent success. But the seed will not sprout and grow under the nurture of a drifter. A drifter is someone who allows life to throw whatever at him and accept it by its appearance. Drifters in the ocean do nothing but drift wherever the ocean takes them. Do not drift through life, but instead TH!NK and swim mindful through all your amazing adventures! Now, Young One, I have a question for you," Jonathan finishes with a pause, looking up at the sky. The tree over them is swiftly waving its branches full of green leaves, as a nice, cool summer breeze passes by. "What soil will you plant these seeds in?"

Nori ponders this question and finally replies, "With a supporting foundation, Soil that will help grow the seed into a strong rooted plant."

"Ah yes—wise answer! Let me add that paying attention to the seeds is equally important as what kind of soil is providing nourishment. The soil that is fertile, will love and support life for the seeds planted in the mind. But the soil that is rough terrain will grow a plant in fear of nutrients and limited life support.

"Nevertheless, the soil you choose will reap the thoughts you sow into the attitude you swim with. An attitude is a cluster of thoughts with emotions attached to each one. Essentially, attitude is the energy of our thoughts."

The sea turtle, lifting his head higher, interrupts with enlightenment: "Our thoughts are the roots, while the effects are the branches, fruits and leaves on the tree."

"Very good use of the sea turtle mindset," Jonathan affirms. "Now my last two questions, and than you are off to travel the world and spread this wisdom."

"I was born ready!" Nori replies enthusiastically.

"If you plant a seed of greatness in fertile loving soil, what kind of emotions would the roots of that seed grow into?"

"Out of love flows joy, beauty, peace, happiness, patience, compassion, kindness, understanding, gentleness, faithfulness, self-discipline, calmness, inspiration, excitement, hope, forgiveness, satisfaction and success."

"Okay. If you plant a seed of greatness in rough terrain soil, what kind of emotions would the roots of that seed grow into?"

"Out of fear runs hate, dislike, anger, ugliness, bitterness, worry, self-pity, envy rage, irritation, unforgiveness, cynicism, unkindness, jealousy, anxiety, dissatisfaction and failure. But like you said, I must pull these weeds from their roots as soon as I notice them!"

"Thats right! The amazing fact that love and fear cannot coexist in our brains at the same time is phenomenal."

"Now my last question for you, Jonathan: Where does love come from, and furthermore, what is love?"

"Love, my son, is everything. All that is alive is connected. Even though you and I are from two different worlds, we are still connected by love. The land loves the sea, as much as the sea loves the land. Love comes from everything, and it is in everything."

"How do you know?" Nori asks his mentor, with curiosity building.

"Well, ask yourself, Are you made out of something, or are you made out of nothing? Let me answer for you—you are something, a sea turtle magnificently created by something, LOVE."

"Where does fear come from?"

"Fear is the opposite of love. Therefore fear is nothing, and comes from nothing."

"Why do I fear sometimes?"

"You have 'learned' to fear, and to create fear when you feel uncomfortable. Learn to love more, and you will fear less. Learn to become comfortable being uncomfortable." Jonathan says as he rises onto his feet.

In that moment, Nori's mind becomes very clear with the lessons he learned that afternoon. All the events of his journey flash through his mind and at the speed of light, he feels connected to all of his thoughts.

"I LOVE everything and fear nothing!" Nori shouts with all his might.

Notes

_____

_____

_____

_____

_____

_____

_____

_____

Words of wisdom… Find yourself a Mentor who has what you want, do what they did to get the same results. This mentor can be someone you personally know, someone from the past or even someone online!

#SeaTurtleMindset

YouTube Chapter Video
http://bit.ly/SeaTurtleMindsetChapter0

ABOUT THE AUTHOR

Jonathan Rosales is a young author and entrepreneur. He is currently passionately involved with helping people gain more fun, freedom, and fulfillment.

Born and raised by Guatemalan immigrant parents in Providence, Rhode Island, he is a big brother to three beautiful sisters and one handsome brother.

He is a first generation college graduate from the University of Rhode Island with a Bachelors Degree in Spanish. During his undergraduate studies he was the President of ESW (Engineers for a Sustainable World), a student organization in which he participated with several other amazing colleagues on humanitarian projects in Guatemala, among them, providing a local school with its first septic tank installation in San Mateo, Huehuetenango, Guatemala.

The profession he has chosen is with an international organization that focuses on finding people who love to travel and help children all around the world. In fact they have even built over 120 bottle schools in Guatemala.

Reach out to the author so he can share with you how to get involved and create an impact with different volunteer projects.

He loves to play soccer every week and aspires to play professionally one day. He also loves to read books every day.

If he is not working hard on his dreams, playing soccer or reading, he is traveling around the world. One of his life goals is to travel to every country around the world (206 to be exact). So far he has traveled well to over 25 states, Spain, Canada, Puerto Rico, Costa Rica, Mexico, South Africa and Guatemala.

If you ever find yourself traveling to Providence, RI (USA). Send him a message on one of his social media accounts. He enjoys making new connections and friends.

Follow Jonathan on Social Media

Facebook: www.fb.com/JonathanLivesLife

Instagram: @JonathanLovesLife

Book Updates | Book Releases | Apparel
www.SeaTurtleMindset.com

Spread Your Wisdom, Stay Connected & Join Other
Sea Turtle Minds Around The World

LIKE
Facebook: www.fb.com/seaturtlemindset

FOLLOW
Instagram: www.instagram.com/seaturtlemindset
Twitter: www.twitter.com/SeaTurtleMind

SUBSCRIBE
YouTube: www.youtube.com/SeaTurtleMindset

Made in the USA
Monee, IL
31 October 2021